For

Rio,

Bo,

Livi,

Sean

and Shannon

… and all kids everywhere!

Book design and illustrations: Diahann Hill
Back cover photograph: Peter Mendelson

Table of Contents

Introduction

The key to enjoying children is knowing what to do with them. This book helps you to unlock the memories of the activities and games that you enjoyed as a child so that you can share them with the next generations.

The Orange Mama Laid will help you remember the words to "This Little Piggy" and the motions to "I'm a Little Teapot", the rules to "Crazy Eights" and "War", how to play "SPUD" and "Kick the Can", and the answer to why a mummy makes a bad gift.

In general, these activities require little or no preparation and few props, and they can be enjoyed by all ages. They'll come in handy when you're suddenly in charge and need some quick ideas for breaking the ice or entertaining the kids, or for pulling them away from their televisions and computers. Best of all, you'll feel more comfortable with the kids when you know how to entertain them, and that's sure to keep them coming back.

As for the title, you'll need to refer to the riddles in the Word Fun section for further explanation.

There are many variations to most of the activities in this book. Avoid spending too much time arguing about the right or wrong way to play them. A little negotiation might be required, but agree on a set of rules and try other variations later. You never know when a new version will be more fun than you expected!

Rhymes and Songs

These activities entertain babies and toddlers by adding hand and body motions to well-known songs and rhymes.

3

S ome of these activities are performed to songs. Use the Internet to find audio samples of the tunes if you are unfamiliar with them.

Five Little Piggies

Holding the bottom of the child's foot toward you, and starting with the big toe, wiggle each toe on his foot for each line in the verse.

For the last line, tickle him by wiggling your index finger down the center of his foot.

This little piggy went to market.
This little piggy stayed home.
This little piggy had roast beef.
This little piggy had none.
This little piggy cried,
"Wee, wee, wee, wee!"
all the way home.

Twinkle, Twinkle, Little Star

Make your hands into fists and then splay them out away from you as though they're flashing, putting each one forward alternately.

Twinkle, twinkle, little star,
How I wonder what you are.

Point up to the sky.

Up above the world so high,

Make a diamond shape with your fingers.

Like a diamond in the sky.

Repeat the twinkling.

Twinkle, twinkle, little star,
How I wonder what you are!

5

Pat-a-Cake

You can perform this rhyme together with a toddler,
or for a baby by gently moving the baby's hands.

Clap the baby's hands together while saying the following:

Pat-a-cake, pat-a-cake, baker's man,
Bake me a cake as fast as you can.

Circle her arms around each other.

Roll it,

Poke one index finger into the opposite palm.

Prick it

Write a "B" in the air with her hand.

And mark it with "B"
And put it...

Lift her hands up.

....way(!) up in the oven for baby and me.

For added drama
— after the first couple of times through the rhyme —
pause before saying, "way!"

You can also do this rhyme with the baby's feet.
It's actually easier since baby hands tend to ball up into little fists.

Here's the Church

Face both palms down so that the fingers are pointing toward each other. Slip them together at the knuckles so that the fingers are intertwined underneath, pointing down. Bring the heels of your hands together so that your fingertips are enclosed between your palms, with your thumbs next to each other in front.

Show the child your hands, with the thumbs in front, and say the following:

Here's the church...

Point both of your index fingers up so that they touch at the tips.

...and here's the steeple

Swing your thumbs to the side.

Open the door...

Open your hands and turn them up, keeping the fingers interlocked and wiggling.

...and see all the people!

The Itsy-Bitsy Spider

Touch the thumb on your left hand to the index finger on your right hand and rotate your right thumb and left index finger upward so that they touch. Repeat in an upward motion to simulate the spider climbing up the spout.

The itsy-bitsy spider climbed up the waterspout.

Spread your fingers out and swoosh your hands down to simulate water rushing down.

Down came the rain and washed the spider out.

Put your arms in a circle over your head, touching hands, to simulate a round sun.

Out came the sun

Lower your hands and then wiggle your fingers as you raise both hands up to simulate the rain evaporating.

And dried up all the rain.

Repeat the first motion of the spider climbing up the spout.

And the itsy-bitsy spider climbed up the spout again.

Do Your Ears Hang Low?

Touch the backs of your hands to your ears with the fingers hanging down while you sing:

Do your ears hang low?

Sway your fingers from side-to-side.

Do they wobble to and fro?

Tie a large knot in the air.

Can you tie them in a knot?

Draw a bow in the air with both hands.

Can you tie them in a bow?

Throw both hands over one shoulder.

Can you throw them over your shoulder...

Salute.

...like a continental soldier?

Touch the backs of your hands to your ears with the fingers hanging down.

Do your ears hang low?

9

I'm a Little Teapot

Sing the following while standing up, with your arms hanging down:

I'm a little teapot, short and stout.

Put your right hand on your hip.

Here is my handle,

Point the left arm and hand out in an "S" shape.

And here is my spout.
When I get all steamed up, hear me shout.

Lean to the left to simulate tea pouring out of your "spout."

Just tip me over and pour me out!

Repeat the tune, while remaining in the shape of the teapot, for the following:

I'm a clever teapot, yes, it's true.
Here's an example of what I can do:

Switch arms.

I can change my handle to my spout.

Repeat pouring motion.

Just tip me over and pour me out!

Ring Around the Rosie

Some toddlers never grow tired of Ring Around the Rosie.
Get the big kids to pitch in because — since it's one of the
few games that they can play together — it makes the toddlers
feel like big kids, too.

Join hands and dance around in a circle, singing the song below.
After the last line, everyone falls down on the ground.

Ring around the rosie,

A pocket full of posies,

Ashes, ashes,

We all fall down!

The Wheels on the Bus

There are lots of verses to this song. You and the kids can make up your own verses as well.

If doing this with a baby or toddler, hold him in your lap as you sing.

Circle the baby's arms around each other.

> *The wheels on the bus go round and round,*
> *round and round, round and round.*
> *The wheels on the bus go round and round,*
> *all through the town.*

Hold the child's forearms straight up and down from the elbows and swing them open and shut.

> *The doors on the bus go open and shut,*
> *open and shut, open and shut.*
> *The doors on the bus go open and shut,*
> *all through the town.*

Hold the child's forearms straight up and down and pivot them from side to side from the elbows.

The wipers on the bus go swish-swish-swish,
swish-swish-swish, swish-swish-swish.
The wipers on the bus go swish-swish-swish,
all through the town.

Make fists with both hands and then splay them out to mimic blinkers.

The blinkers on the bus go blink-blink-blink,
blink-blink-blink, blink-blink-blink.

The blinkers on the bus go blink-blink-blink,
all through the town.

Gently bounce the baby (or gently pick her up and down
if she's not on your lap).

The people on the bus bump up and down,
up and down, up and down.
The people on the bus bump up and down,
all through the town.

Give the baby a hug.

The mommies (or aunties, grannies, etc.) on the bus say,
"I love you. I love you. I love you."
The mommies on the bus say, "I love you,"
all through the town.

Miss Mary Mack

Miss Mary Mack is for the older kids; it requires older-kid coordination and memorization.

Two players sit cross-legged, facing each other, saying the rhyme below. The same motions are used for each line in this rhyme.

For the first word, each player slaps her upper arms with her opposite hands.

For the second word, each player slaps her legs.

Where dashes are displayed in the second word, the two syllables should be counted as separate words.

For the third word, each player claps her own hands.

For the remaining words, each player slaps the opposite player's same hand (right palm slaps right palm), claps her own hands (without saying a word), and then claps the other hand with the opposite player (left palm slaps left palm), until the end of the line.

Repeat for each line in the verse below:

> *Miss Mar-y Mack, Mack, Mack*
> *All dressed in black, black, black*
> *With sil-ver buttons, buttons, buttons*
> *All down her back, back, back*
> *She asked her mother, mother, mother*
> *For fif-ty cents, cents, cents*
> *To see the elephants, elephants, elephants*
> *Jump over the fence, fence, fence*
> *They jumped so high, high, high*
> *They touched the sky, sky, sky*
> *And didn't come back, back, back*
> *Till the Fourth of July, July, July*

Repeat, speeding up each time, until the players make a mistake.

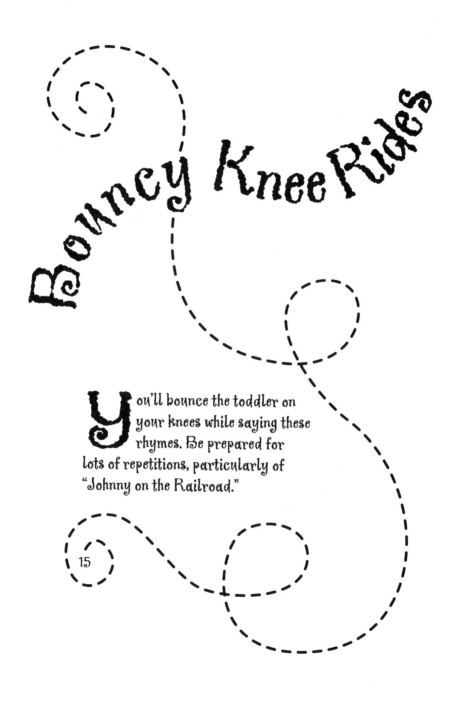

Bouncy Knee Rides

You'll bounce the toddler on your knees while saying these rhymes. Be prepared for lots of repetitions, particularly of "Johnny on the Railroad."

15

Johnny on the Railroad

Gently bounce the toddler on
your lap while holding him
securely around the waist.
On the word "hole," open
your lap and lower the child
— quickly but gently —
to the ground.

Johnny on the railroad,
Picking up coal —
Along comes an engine that knocks
him down the hole!

For added suspense, after the
first time or two, pause before
saying "hole." The child will
get squirmy in anticipation
of falling in the hole.

This is How the Ladies Ride

Use a sing-song voice for this rhyme.

Gently bounce the child on your lap while holding her securely around the waist, in rhythm to the "trot, trot, trot."

> *This is the way the ladies ride: trot, trot, trot.*

Continue to bounce the child gently, but say the line and bounce her a little faster and higher.

> *This is the way the gentlemen ride: gallop, gallop, gallop.*

Lift your knees up even higher, in rhythm with the "Giddyup."

> *This is the way the farmers ride: Giddyup! Giddyup! Giddyup!*

Alternately raise, lower, and wiggle your knees so that the child wobbles between them.

> *And this is the way the hobos ride:*
> *a hobbledy dee dee, a hobbledy dee dee!*

The Noble Duke of York

Sit on the floor so that your legs are extended in front of you and place the child at the edge of your lap, near your knees. You may want to lean against a wall to brace your back.

Gently bounce the child on your lap.

> *Oh, the noble Duke of York!*
> *He had ten thousand men.*

Gently bounce your knees up, a little higher each time.

> *He marched them up to the top of the hill and*

Gently bounce your knees down again, a little lower each time.

> *Marched them down again.*

Lift your knees up.

> *And when you're up, you're up,*

Drop your knees down.

> *And when you're down, you're down,*

Lift your knees halfway.

> *And when you're only half way up,*

Lift your knees up and down.

> *You're neither up nor down.*

19

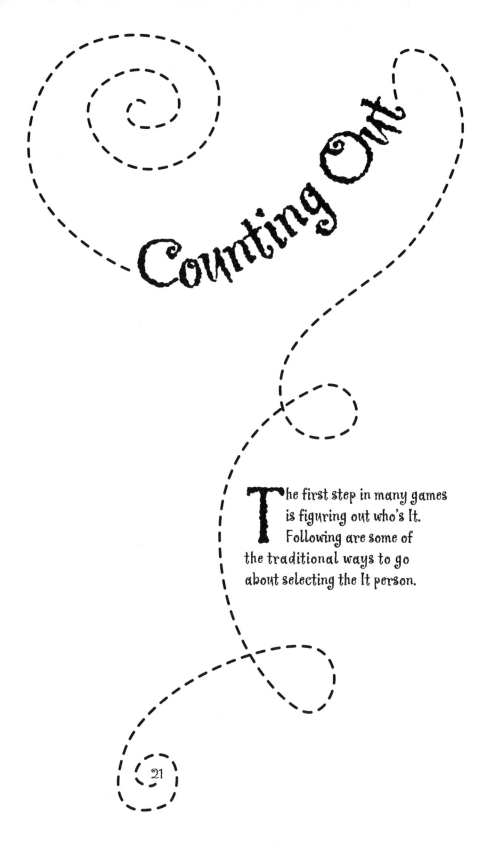

Counting Out

The first step in many games is figuring out who's It. Following are some of the traditional ways to go about selecting the It person.

For each of the following rhymes, the players form a circle and each person puts a fist into the middle of the circle.

The person who's counting goes around the circle, tapping his other fist on top of each player's fist to the rhythm of the verse. The person whose fist is tapped on the last word of the rhyme is out.

The rhyme repeats until only one person — the It person — is left.

If there are only a few players, everyone can put both fists into the circle. Since the counter still needs a fist to count with, he uses his chin as his second fist. He bops himself gently under the . chin when counting around the circle.

Eenie, Meenie, Meinie, Moe

The counter says the following as he taps fists around the circle:

Eenie, meenie, meinie, moe,
Catch a tiger by the toe.
If he hollers, let him go,
Eenie, meenie, meinie, moe.

My mother told me to choose the very best one,
and you are not It.

One Potato

The counter says the following as he taps fists around the circle:

One potato, two potato, three potato, four,
Five potato, six potato, seven potato, more.

Engine No. 9

The counter says the following as she taps fists around the circle:

Engine, engine, number nine,
Going down Chicago line.

If the train falls off the track,
Do you want your money back?

The player whose fist she has landed on will say, "Yes" or "No."

The counter then spells the answer as follows, still tapping her fist around the circle:

N-o spells "no," and you are not it.
– or –
Y-e-s spells "yes," and you are not it.

This one is done with feet instead of fists.

Everyone sits or kneels down and puts one foot into a circle.
The counter will go around the circle, tapping his fist on each
person's foot for each word in the rhyme.

Bubblegum, bubblegum in a dish,
How many pieces do you wish?

Whoever's foot the counter lands on will say a number less than 20.
The counter then counts that number around the circle.

Not It!

The easiest way to figure out who's It is for one person to holler, "Last one to say, 'Not It' is It," after which he and everyone shouts, "Not It!" The last person to say, "Not It" is It.

This may not seem particularly fair but the kids like it, and it seems to work. For a lot of games, being It is half the fun.

Rock Paper Scissors

Even adults will use this method for resolving disputes and determining responsibility.

This is typically played by two people, but can be played by more. It's usually played "best out of three," where one person has to win twice out of three tries.

Each person makes a fist and moves it up and down as she counts to three. On the third count, each person makes her fist into a rock (leave it as a fist), a pair of scissors (hold the index and middle fingers out in a V) or a piece of paper (hand is flat).

The winner is determined as follows: rock smashes scissors; scissors cut paper; paper covers a rock.

Hide and Seek

If you're playing these games with little children and you're the seeker, make lots of noise and say out loud where you're looking. Their giggles will often give them away; they usually can't wait to be found, but they love knowing that you're looking and not finding them.

The very littlest tend to reuse the same spot turn after turn. The older players should help the younger players find new hiding places, and the It person might want to avoid looking in previous hiding spots until she's looked around for a bit.

For all of these games, make sure that the boundaries are well defined and that the players have agreed to what number the It person must count before she can start seeking people. One way to pace the counting is to use a word such as "alligator," "hippopotamus" or "Mississippi" between numbers.

If the seeker can't find everyone and gives up, she shouts, "Ollie, Ollie, in come free!" All of the players must return to base when they hear this.

There are many different opinions on the exact wording of this phrase — and just as many theories on its origin. Don't waste too much time arguing about the correct way to say it!

Hide-and-Seek

Identify a "base" where the It person will count and to which the hiders will be sent when they are found.

While the It person is counting out loud with her eyes covered, everyone runs to a hiding place, where they stay for the remainder of the game. When the It person is finished counting, she says, "Ready or not, here I come!"

The It person tries to find all of the players. When a player is found, he's sent to base. The first person found is It the next time.

Sardines

Sardines is the opposite of Hide-and-Seek. In this game, the players are trying to find the It person. Sardines is especially fun for the big kids when played in the dark; the little kids might find the dark a bit too scary. The game gets spookier and spookier as the players silently melt away into their hiding places until only one seeker is left…

The It person hides while everyone else counts, keeping their eyes closed (if playing inside, the seekers can shut themselves in a bathroom or closet while counting). When the seekers have finished counting, they holler, "Ready or not, here we come!"

Everyone spreads out and searches for the It person. When someone finds the It person — and when the coast is clear of other players — he climbs into the hiding spot with her, or as close as he can get and still be hidden.

Continue playing until everyone has found the It person.

The first person to find the It person is It the next time.

Piggy Wants a Signal

This game is like Hide-and-Seek except that a captured player may be freed from base and return to hiding.

Like Hide-and-Seek, the seeker counts and the other players hide. However, once a player has been captured and returns to base, he hollers, "Piggy wants a signal!" When another player responds with a snorting sound like a pig, the captured player is free to hide again, when the It person isn't looking.

The game ends when all of the players have been found or when one person has been captured three times. The person who was found three times, or else the first person captured, is It the next time.

"Piggy Wants a Signal" can also be played as "Piggy Wants a Motion," where players must make a motion instead of a snorting sound to free a captured player. The captured player can escape only when he sees a motion made by another player.

This game is most fun at night; it typically requires players to move around so that they can be seen by the "piggy" in the dark, making it riskier and more exciting.

Tag

33

For tag games, like the hide-and-seek games, agree ahead of time on the boundaries and the number to which the It person must count before he may start chasing the other players.

Freeze Tag

In Freeze Tag, when the It person tags someone, that person becomes frozen in the position in which she was tagged and can't move until somebody else tags her. Then she becomes free to run around again.

The first player tagged three times becomes It and the game is repeated.

Tunnel Tag

Tunnel tag is entertaining when mixing age groups since crawling through the tunnels (legs) of the smaller players can be a squeeze for the bigger players — and the free person has to squeeze through quickly or risk being caught. Be prepared for grass stains!

When the It person tags someone while playing Tunnel Tag, the tagged person makes his legs into a tunnel and can't run until somebody else crawls through the tunnel.

Like Freeze Tag, he is then free to run around again, and the first person tagged three times becomes It.

The It person may tag a person who is crawling through another person's legs. Then that person must also make a tunnel.

This version of tag is also referred to as Stuck in the Mud.

Immunity Tag

A few creative ideas for "immunity" can make for a lot of laughs in this game. But note that the players have to use immunity sparingly.

For Immunity Tag, everyone agrees on an action that will make players "immune" to the It person. For example, the players might agree that a cartwheel — or a pirouette, or lying on your back like a stuck turtle or imitating a chicken — will make a player immune. The It person may not tag a person who is immune.

Immunity lasts for only three seconds, during which time the It person must go after another player and the immune player may run away.

The first person tagged — or to be immune three times — is It.

You can also use categories for immunity. A popular version is "TV Tag," which requires the player to name a TV show in order to be immune.

Sticky Fingers Tag

This version of tag will test the coordination of the runners, especially if the It person is strategic when tagging players.

When the It person tags a player, the tagged person must put a hand on the place on her body where she was tagged — and she must leave it there until a new person becomes It.

If she is tagged again, she must put her other hand on that spot and continue to run.

If she is tagged a third time, she becomes It.

The It person may not tag a person twice in a row without first trying to tag someone else.

Budge Tag

This and Elbow Tag require less running around for the It person since the It person only needs to tag somebody once. Needless to say, this is a boon to the older folks!

Three or four bases — such as baseball bases, trees or lawn chairs — are designated as safety bases; when a player is standing on or touching a base, the It person may not tag that person.

However, only one person may be on each base at time. As a player runs toward a base, he may shout, "Budge!", in which case the player currently on the base must leave it.

The first player tagged becomes It, and the game is repeated.

There should be fewer bases than players, and the fewer bases there are, the more exciting the game.

Amoeba Tag

Amoeba Tag — which is also called Blob Tag — will test the players' teamwork abilities.

When the It person tags someone, the tagged player joins hands with the It person and can also tag players. This continues until the last player is left, who becomes It. Only the head and tail of the amoeba (the first and last people in the line) may actually tag other players.

Elbow Tag

Elbow tag is an excellent icebreaker because it involves a little physical bonding with other players.

In this game, there is an It person and a free person (or two free people if playing with an odd number of players). Everyone else is in pairs around the lawn, joined by hooking one elbow each.

The It person tries to tag the free person. However, when the free person joins elbows with one of the members of a pair, the other person in the original pair is now the free person. The original free person is safe and the new free person needs to run.

When the It person tags the free person, the free person becomes It and the game is repeated.

With younger kids, you'll often need to remind them to let go of the pair once you've joined it. Make sure the bigger kids know to help with this.

What Time is it Mr. Fox?

One player — Mr. Fox — stands at one end of the lawn or driveway, with his back to the other players. The other players — the chickens — are behind a line about 20 paces away, facing Mr. Fox.

All of the chickens shout, "What time is it, Mr. Fox?"

Mr. Fox responds with a time, for example, "2 o'clock." All of the chickens must take a step for each hour (two, in this case) in response. The size of the steps is up to the chickens but the first chicken to get close enough to Mr. Fox will tag him and become the new fox. At that point, the game starts over with the new Mr. Fox.

However, when the chickens ask what time it is, Mr. Fox may respond, "Dinner time!" and chase all of the chickens back to the starting line. If he tags any chickens before they reach the starting line, the tagged chickens sit out the rest of the game. Mr. Fox then goes back to his end and turns around to repeat the dialogue with the chickens.

Unless one of the chickens tags Mr. Fox first, the last chicken left becomes Mr. Fox and the game starts over.

You may decide that any chickens that are caught become foxes, too. They return with Mr. Fox to his end and also turn their backs. When Mr. Fox yells, "Dinner time!", they all turn around to chase the chickens. If a chicken tags any of the foxes before "Dinner time", or is the last one left, that chicken becomes the new Mr. Fox.

Tag with a Twist

These games combine Tag with Hide-and-Seek and other twists.

L ike the previous games,
make sure that the boundaries
and count are agreed to.

Kick the Can

This game requires a can about the size of a coffee can.

A can is placed upright on the ground, and an area nearby — such as a rock or a tree — is designated as the jail.

The It person closes his eyes and counts while the other players hide. When the It person finishes counting, he hollers, "Ready or not, here I come!"

The It person looks for the other players. When he sees one, he says the player's name and races that person to the can (if he says the wrong name, the player can stay in hiding). If the It person kicks the can over before the other player (the hider) gets to it, the hider must go to jail.

However, if the hider kicks over the can before the It person does, the game starts again. The can is replaced upright on the ground, and the It person counts again while everyone else, including the players in jail, scatters and hides.

Players are expected to move around while they're hiding and may free everyone in jail by sneaking up and kicking the can before the It person tags them. If the It person tags a player, she must go to jail; otherwise, the It person counts again and everyone else scatters and hides.

The goal is for the It person to see or tag all of the players before they can be freed from jail; the first person captured is It the next time.

Capture the Flag

Capture the Flag combines Tag with stealth and strategy. It's the game behind Paintball and Laser Tag.

Ideally, Capture the Flag is played in the woods. The two teams should not be able to see each other when they hide their flags.

There are many variations to this game, so be sure that everyone understands and agrees to the rules.

The playing area must be clearly defined and split in half. Each team designates a jail at the back of its side of the playing area, typically a tree or rock or other object.

Both teams have a flag (a brightly-colored bandanna or old T-shirt) which they place somewhere on their side of the field. The flag must be between knee- and eye-level and be partially visible. When both teams have hidden their flags (they can holler or whistle when they're finished, or be allocated a set amount of time), the game begins.

The object is to capture the other team's flag and bring it back to your side of the field. However, whenever a player is on the other team's side of the field, the player may be tagged and must go directly to the opponent's jail.

A player can only be freed from jail (a "jailbreak") if someone else on his team tags him while he's in jail. The freed person must return to his side before he may be tagged or continue playing the game.

The winning team is the one that captures the other team's flag — or all of the other team's players — first.

A certain amount of time should be allocated (typically 20 – 30 minutes), after which the game is a draw if neither team has won.

A few additional rules and tips:

▌ Captured players may not yell any information to their teammates.

▌ The flag must be carried to the other side; it may not be thrown over the line. It can be handed off to another team member as long as the first person has not been tagged.

▌If a person carrying the flag is tagged, the flag is dropped at the point where the player was captured. (One variation requires that the flag be returned to the original hiding place.)

▌Neither team may move its own flag once play has begun.

Typically, the teams will divide into defenders, who stay on their side to catch attackers from the other side, and attackers, who go after the other flag. Depending upon how many attackers are caught from their side, the defenders should be prepared to become attackers as the game progresses.

A simpler version of this game can be played by using two clearly visible flags at each end of a field or lawn. Then it becomes a game of tag rather than stealth.

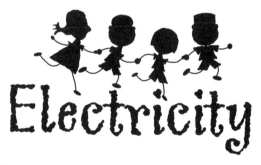

Electricity

Whenever jailbreaks are part of the game, such as with Capture the Flag, the teams should agree whether captured players may use "electricity" to be freed.

Electricity means that captured players may join hands to form lines that extend out of jail — so long as one player is in or touching the jail — and that everyone is freed if anyone is tagged by a free player.

When the base is a safety base, rather than a jail, electricity may also be used to extend safety. In this case, the safe players may join hands in order to make it easier for other players to reach safety.

Spotlight Tag

Spotlight Tag is played at night. Be sure not to alarm neighbors and people passing by as you sneak around!

You'll need one or two flashlights for this game.

Before starting, designate an area — such as a front porch — as the jail.

The It person counts while everyone runs and hides within the agreed-to boundaries.

The It person captures people by shining the flashlight on them and calling out the correct name. When a player is captured, he is sent to jail. Meanwhile, all of the other players may move about as much as they'd like.

At this point, there are two common ways to play this game:

▌Keep playing until the It person has captured all of the players. The first person captured is It in the next game.

▌Play with one or two It people and a jail. Other players are allowed to tag prisoners in jail, which sets them free to run and hide again. Only the prisoners who are actually tagged may run free, unless everyone agrees to allow electricity to be used for jailbreaks. Typically, the second It person stays close to the jail to prevent any jailbreaks. Play continues until all players are captured or one player is captured three times.

Ghosts in the Graveyard

This game is also played at night, when the ghosts are out. Dim flashlights may be necessary if there isn't a full moon or streetlights.

The It person — the ghost — hides within the designated area while the rest of the players stay on base and count. They count by shouting, "One o'clock! Two o'clock!" until they get to "Midnight! I hope I don't see a ghost tonight!"

Once the seekers have counted to midnight, they start searching for the ghost. As soon as someone sees the ghost, she points and hollers, "Ghost in the graveyard!"

At that point, the ghost gives a ghostly scream and everyone runs to base while the ghost tries to tag them. The ghost tries to catch as many people as he can. Whomever he tags first is It the next time. If he doesn't tag anyone, the game is replayed.

"Bloody Murder" is essentially the same game, without the ghostly aspects. In this game, the players shout, "Bloody Murder" when they see the It person.

Ghosts in the Graveyard II

In this variation of Ghost in the Graveyard, the ghost is allowed to ambush the seekers, but she must still give the ghostly scream so that everyone knows she's there.

When she does scream, all the seekers run to base and the ghost tags as many players as she can. All of the tagged players are also ghosts the next time. As soon as one of them screams, they all must start screaming and chasing the seekers.

The game is repeated until one person is left; that person is the ghost for the next round.

The ambush potential adds a thrill to this version of the game. A clever ghost will wait until several people are nearby before pouncing.

Races

49

These races require almost no preparation and even adults will find them entertaining. Only a few players are needed for most of them.

For all of these races, the participants line up at one end of the playing area and the goal is to be the first player or team to reach the opposite end of the playing area.

It's always best to have one person who's not participating in the race watch to see who the winner is. That person will usually kick off the race by saying, "On your mark! Get set! Go!"

If there is an even number of players, you can turn the races into relay races. The players pair up and each member of the pair lines up across from the other at opposite ends of the field. The players at one end (the starting line) will race toward their partners at the other end. When they reach their partners, they will touch ("tag off") their partners, who will then race back to the starting line.

Wheelbarrow Race

One player — the wheelbarrow — lies face-down on the grass, with his hands on the ground next to his shoulders. The other player picks the wheelbarrow's feet up about waist-high and the wheelbarrow lifts his body off of the ground so that he is essentially walking on his hands.

If doing relay races, have team members switch positions when they get to the other end of the field.

Crab Walk Race

All players sit on the ground with their knees bent and feet planted on the ground in front of them. They put their hands on the ground behind them and lift their rear ends off the ground so that they are walking on their feet and hands with their stomachs facing up. Players race backward (head first).

Spider Race

Two players stand
back-to-back and
link elbows. They
then run sideways
together to the goal.

Wiggle Worm Race

Two players
face the goal,
one behind the other.
The player in front puts
her left hand back through
her legs; the player in back
holds her hand with his right
hand. This can also be played
with teams of more than two people.

Bear Walk Race

Players race forward on all fours, except that they are not allowed to bend their knees or elbows.

Wacky-Walk Race

Each player must carry a Frisbee or other object between his knees. If he drops the object, he must stop, pick it up and place it back between his knees before he can continue; or you can disqualify a player who drops the object.

Racers may find that jumping is easier; but since it's not nearly as much fun for the spectators, decide whether or not to allow it.

Jamaquack Race

Jamaquacks are (imaginary) rare birds from Australia.

For this race, all players turn their backs to the goal, bend over, grab their ankles and look through their legs as they race backward to the goal.

This makes an especially fun relay race since the tag-off is done by bumping bums. You can also do a three-legged variation in which partners stand side-by-side and hold the ankle of one another's inside leg, as well as their own outside legs.

Optionally, players may squawk like jamaquacks as they waddle down the field.

Other Lawn Games

Follow the Leader

Toddlers can provide all kinds of entertainment if you can get them to follow along to this game. Bigger kids will have fun devising the most ridiculous moves they can think of. You'll get some laughs, too, if any other adults are watching. Remember: You have to do whatever the leader does!

There are no real rules to this game. Everyone forms a line and has to do whatever the person in front does as they move about the room or yard. You can use a distance (such as once around the yard) to decide when to switch leaders.

Duck Duck Goose

Everyone sits in a circle facing each other.

The Goose walks around behind the circle, tapping each person on the head, saying, "Duck" each time. However, when he taps someone on the head and says, "Goose," that person must jump up and chase the Goose around the circle, trying to tag him.

If the old Goose runs around the circle and sits down in the now-empty spot in the circle before the new Goose tags him, the game is repeated with the new Goose. However, if the new Goose tags the old Goose before he sits down, the new Goose gets to sit, the old Goose remains It, and the game is repeated.

Simon Says

Like other activities, silly ideas will make this game a lot more memorable.

One person is Simon and stands facing the other players, who are also standing.

Simon gives commands such as "Simon says to put your thumb in your ear" or "hum 'Twinkle, Twinkle, Little Star',," which all the players must do. However, if Simon doesn't say "Simon says" first, the players are NOT supposed to obey the command; any that do are out of the game.

The last person left becomes Simon for the next game.

Mother, May I?

One person is the "Mother" and stands about 20 feet away from the other players, who are lined up next to each other. Mother has her back to the other players.

Mother calls out the name of a player and gives various commands, such as "Take three giant steps," after which the named player must say, "Mother, may I?" Mother may respond with either "yes," in which case the player follows the command, or "no," in which case she doesn't. However, if the player doesn't remember to ask first, she goes all the way back to the starting line.

The first player to tag Mother wins and becomes Mother.

The commands usually include the following, but feel free to add your own:

Baby steps

Giant steps

Regular steps

Bunny steps (hops)

Banana steps ⌣ For each step, you lie down, putting your feet where your head was in the previous step.

Mother can also tell the players to go either forward or backward.

Red Light

Like Mother, May I? one person plays the "stoplight" and stands about 20 feet in front of the other players, who are lined up next to each other.

Green Light

The Stoplight turns away from the other players and says, "Green light!" at which point all the other players race toward the Stoplight. However, when the Stoplight says, "Red light!" and turns around, none of the other players may be moving. Any who are moving are out.

Play continues until everybody is out — or until a player tags the Stoplight, in which case that player becomes the new Stoplight.

You may want to require one or two seconds ("one alligator, two alligator") for the players to freeze before the Stoplight turns around. The game has the potential to get contentious if the runners think the Stoplight is turning around too quickly or judging too harshly.

Doctor! Doctor!

One player is the Doctor and must turn around so that he cannot see the other players.

The other players form a circle, holding hands, and then step over and under each other to form a human knot, never letting go of each other's hands.

When they are all tangled up, they call, "Doctor! Doctor! Please help!"

The Doctor turns around and has to untangle the knot by telling everyone where and what to move, without their letting go of each other's hands.

Red Rover

An advantage to this game is that everyone ends up a winner.

The players divide into two teams and line up with arms linked, facing each other about 20 feet apart. The first team will pick a player on the opposing team — Timmy, for example — and holler, "Red Rover! Red Rover! Send Timmy over!"

Timmy will run to the other line and try to break through the arms of the players. If he succeeds, he gets to pick one person from that team and bring her over to his team.

If he does not succeed, he joins the other team.

Timmy's original team takes a turn calling on one of the players from the other team; each team alternates turns until all players are on one team.

Water Balloon Toss

A water balloon toss is always
a favorite on a hot day since there's a
good chance of somebody getting wet. Water
balloon fights are even better, but be careful since
the balloons can sting when they hit.

Pairs face each other a few feet apart, with one person in
each pair holding a balloon full of water. All at the same time,
the people holding the balloons toss them to their partners.

Once the partners have caught the balloons, everybody takes
a step backward and repeats the toss. If someone drops
the balloon, he may pick it up to complete the toss.

Once the teams are far enough apart — and depending
on how full the balloons are — the balloons will start
popping when they're dropped. The last pair with
a whole balloon wins.

Some kids will care about their times running an obstacle course and some won't. Adults will have fun setting them up — and might even find the competitor in themselves as well. Best of all, the courses can be very simple and still be fun.

To make obstacle courses, use sticks to make hurdles in the lawn; set up a hula hoop through which a football has to be tossed; put out chairs that have to be crawled under; use chalk to draw circles that must be hopped through; include a "bat race" (stand the business end of the bat on the ground and lower the forehead until it touches the handle, then spin around the bat 3 times and continue); set up small cones that must be run around. Just look around, see what you have to work with and use your imagination!

Each competitor will take a turn running the course from start to finish and is timed using a stopwatch. The one with the lowest time wins.

You can dock the competitors some number of seconds if they knock over a hurdle, chair or other obstacle. You may also want to give them three tries to accomplish a goal (such as getting a ball through a hoop) and let them continue if they're unsuccessful.

Blowing Grass

This is an activity that will impress the kids for a simple reason: It's loud.

Take a long strand of grass — the sturdier the better — and hold the bottom of it between the bases of your thumbs, flat side to each thumb. Pull the top with your index fingers so that it is taut and pinch it in the middle between the tops of your thumbs.

The two thumbs are side-by-side and the piece of grass is a straight, taut line between them. Put your mouth up to your thumbs and blow. It may take a few tries, but you should eventually unleash a loud whistle.

Playground Games

These are games for asphalt or concrete playgrounds. They require big outdoor chalk for drawing lines and/or a bouncy playground ball. They may also require pebbles.

65

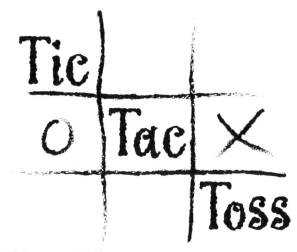

Tic
O Tac X
Toss

This game is the same as Tic-Tac-Toe, but is played on the ground with pebbles and chalk. Each player must have her own pebble.

Draw two perpendicular sets of parallel lines, just as you would for Tic-Tac-Toe.

The players decide who will use X's and who will use O's.

Each player takes turns tossing her pebble into a square. If the pebble lands in a square, the player chalks an "X" or an "O," as appropriate. If a pebble lands in a square that already has a mark in it, on a line or outside of all of the squares, the player loses her turn.

The goal is to be the first player to get three X's or O's in a row, up-and-down, across or diagonally.

Hopscotch

For Hopscotch, each player must have a pebble to use as a marker.

Using chalk, draw out squares, about a foot square each, as drawn here. Draw a half-circle at the top.

The first player tosses her marker into square 1. If it lands outside of the square (decide whether it's okay if it lands on a line), the turn is forfeited. If the marker lands within the square, the player hops through the squares.

She hops on one foot into each of the squares, skipping the square holding her stone and putting both feet down at once in squares 4/5 and 7/8, unless her marker happens to be in one of these. In the top half-circle, she can put both feet down, turn around and hop back through the squares the same way. On the way back, she must pick up her marker while she's on the square just before the square with the marker. She may not touch the ground with her other foot or put her hands on the ground while doing this.

If she makes it all the way back without stepping on a line, missing a square, landing in the square with the marker or losing her balance, she starts over, trying to toss her marker into square 2. Otherwise, she loses her turn.

The first player to reach square 9 and successfully hop through that turn wins.

To make the game a little easier for the smaller kids, just draw to the number six, with the half-circle after that.

FOUR Square

This game requires a bouncy playground ball.

Start by drawing a big square (at least 10 feet across) with chalk on the ground and dividing it in half both ways so that it becomes four even-sized squares. Number each square clockwise from 1 to 4.

Each player stands in a square. The player in square 4 serves the ball by bouncing it once in his square and then hitting it into another square. The receiving player must let the ball bounce once in her square and then hit it into another square, using one hand or both hands together (double-hits are illegal). Play continues until the hitter hits the ball out of bounds, a receiver is hit by the ball or fails to hit it, or does not let it bounce exactly once before she hits it.

When a player loses, she moves to square 1, and the other players move up a number. The goal is to stay in square 4 as long as possible. If playing with more than four players, a player who loses goes to the end of the line, and the person at the front of the line moves into square 1.

Players may step out of their squares when hitting or receiving the ball.

A twist to this game is to play with categories. The person in square 4 calls out a category — for example, "Car brands" or "Cartoon characters" — as he serves. Each player must name an item from that category whenever he hits the ball. If a player fails to do so before the ball lands in the receiver's square, he's out.

SPUD

This game also requires a bouncy playground ball.

The players assign numbers to themselves by counting off from 1.

The It person throws the ball straight up in the air and calls the number of one of the other players. The person with that number tries to catch the ball before it hits the ground while all of the other players run away from the ball as fast as they can. If the person whose number was called catches the ball, she will throw it up and call the number of a different player.

However, if the ball bounces, she shouts "SPUD!" when she catches the ball and all players must stop running. She takes four giant steps — spelling S-P-U-D — toward the closest player and tries to hit that person with the ball. The targeted player may not move his feet while dodging the ball, but he may catch the ball.

If the It person hits the other player, the player gets a point and becomes It. If the It person misses or if the other player catches the ball, the It person gets a point and remains It.

The It person throws up the ball, calling a different number, and the game repeats.

Each point is used to spell S-P-U-D. When a person gets SPUD, she is out of the game. Play continues until one person is left and that person is the winner.

For a little more difficulty, players may also assign themselves random numbers. If a player throws the ball up and can't remember a valid number before the ball hits the ground, he gets a point and has to throw it again.

Smaug's Treasure

Smaug is the fire-breathing dragon in J.R.R. Tolkien's *The Hobbit* from whom Bilbo Baggins must retrieve the dwarves' stolen treasure.

A bandanna, ball, hat or similar object is used to represent the treasure that Smaug is hiding.

Use chalk to draw a large circle. Place the treasure into the middle of the circle. Smaug stands inside the circle, over the treasure, and the other players stand outside the circle. Smaug may not stand or sit on the treasure, or pick it up.

When Smaug shouts, "Go!" all of the other players try to steal the treasure and take it back outside the circle. If Smaug tags a player, the player must go back outside the circle; if the player is holding the treasure, he must return it to the center of the circle.

The person who succeeds in stealing the treasure and bringing it outside the circle without being tagged becomes Smaug in the next game.

You can also play that a person becomes frozen if she is tagged. Smaug wins and is Smaug again if nobody captures the treasure before all of the other players become frozen.

Swimming Pool Games

Before playing this game, agree whether or not players — including the It person — may swim underwater. Since a player won't necessarily hear the "Marco" underwater, it can make for some disagreements as to what's fair.

The It person submerges himself, holds up one hand and uses his fingers to count to five.

At that point, he comes to the surface with his eyes closed and calls out, "Marco." All the other players must call out, "Polo." The It person must keep his eyes closed and chase the other players around the pool until he tags another player, who becomes the It person.

Whenever the It person hollers, "Marco," all the other players must holler, "Polo" — even if they're right next to the It person!

Kids can spend hours in the pool playing this game.

The "Shark" starts in the middle of the pool, typically in the deep end. All the other players are "minnows" and start out of the water on one side of the pool.

When the Shark calls out, "Minnows!", the minnows jump or dive into the pool and try to swim to the other side and get out without being tagged by the Shark. If they are tagged, they become sharks and stay in the water to help catch the other minnows.

The game is played again until there is only one minnow left. This minnow is the winner and is the Shark in the next game.

Tag

Many of the versions of Tag
described earlier in this book can
be played in the shallow end of the
pool. Tunnel Tag, which is usually
called Stuck in the Mud when
played in the pool, is the
most common.

Any category may be used for this game. Instead of colors,
you may choose to use animals, action heroes, etc.

The It person stands at one end of the pool, facing away
from the pool. The other players are in the pool, hanging
onto the wall closest to the It person.

The players take a few moments to decide on a color,
but they don't say it aloud. After a minute or so, the
It person will ask, "Does everyone have their colors?"
to which everyone usually responds that they do.

The It person then starts calling out colors. If she calls
somebody's color, that person or people must start
swimming to the other end of the pool as quietly
as they can.

If the It person hears them, she jumps in and if she
catches one of them, that person becomes It.

Play continues until the It person tags someone in
the pool. If everyone gets to the other side before she
catches them, the game begins again and she's It again.

Searching Games

Treasure Hunts

Treasure hunts require some preparation, but they are a big win with the kids and are great for around the house, around the yard and around the neighborhood. They're fun on special occasions or for no reason at all. You can play with one team or several teams, depending upon how many kids are playing.

To prepare for a treasure hunt, you create identical sets of clues, one for each team. Each clue leads the team to the location of the next clue; the last clue takes the team to the location of the treasure, which is hidden ahead of time.

Make sure to place the clues in a different order for each team so that they're not following each other around. You start both teams at the same time by giving each team its first clue.

The winner is the team that finds the hidden treasure first. Even with just one team, you'll still have a winning team!

Especially when playing with smaller kids, you may want to hide as many treasures as there are teams and have each team pick which one they want as they find it; then everybody wins. Make sure that everyone on the team will be able to share the treasure.

The clues are the real fun in the treasure hunt. You can use rhyming clues, silly non-rhyming clues, fill-in-the-blank clues (rhyming or not), picture games, word jumbles, hidden words (the words are hidden in a grid of letters), etc. Be sure to put the clues in no logical physical order so that the teams are running upstairs, downstairs and back upstairs again. Depending upon how much space you have, this game can tire a team out!

Scavenger Hunt

Scavenger hunts also require a degree of resourcefulness and preparation, but they can keep the kids busy for good stretches of time.

The hunt needs to be adjusted to the age of the players; it may be confined to a yard or home for younger kids, or to a neighborhood for older kids. Adults enjoy the hunts, too, and will often roam a whole city in search of their treasures.

Like treasure hunts, players are organized into one or more teams. The organizer will identify a list of things that each team must gather (each team gets the same list) and how much time they are allowed to complete the list; the first team to gather all of the objects in the allotted time wins.

For smaller kids, the list might include "something fuzzy" and "something pink," or outlines of their hands on pieces of paper. You'll likely need a bigger kid or adult on each team for supervision and guidance, and that person should keep the kids wound up by reminding them that it's a race. Little kids have little concept of winning, but will still jump all over the place if you make it sound exciting.

For bigger kids, you may want to provide digital cameras so that they can fulfill tasks such as making a pyramid in front of some nearby landmark, or all fitting into a small space.

For adults…well, that's a subject for a different book!

Hot Cold

This game can be used any time a child is trying to find something; often times, pointing and directions just don't do the trick.

If playing with two people, the It person will select an object and the other person — the seeker — will try to find it.

As the seeker moves around the room, the It person will tell the seeker whether he's "cold" or "getting colder" if he's far or moving away from the object; "warm," "getting warmer" or "getting hotter" if the seeker is getting closer to the object; and "hot" if the seeker is very near to the object.

Walking Games

83

There's only one game in this
category, but no childhood
is complete without it.

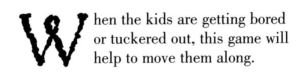

W hen the kids are getting bored or tuckered out, this game will help to move them along.

Step on a Crack

This game begins when someone says, "Step on a crack, break your mother's back!" or "Step on a line, break your mother's spine!"

Once this has been said, nobody is allowed to step on any cracks in the sidewalk. The winner is the last one to step on a crack. Typically, no one is really verifying who's winning or losing; it tends to be more of a personal challenge.

Some people prefer to substitute "the camel's" for "your mother's."

If you're hiking instead of walking on city streets, you can still play a similar game, where no one is allowed to touch the ground. In this case, only rocks, roots, twigs and such things may be stepped on. A player's foot may touch the ground but must be mostly on the other objects. If you think up reasons for not touching the ground, such as its being boiling lava or an ocean full of evil creatures, the kids will be much less interested in who's winning or losing and much more interested in everyone getting back on "safe ground."

Car Games

When you're
the relative
squeezed into
the back of a minivan
full of kids, these games
can be sanity-savers,
peace-keepers and
time-gobblers.

I Spy

This game is easy for the smallest children to play. However, the eyes are focused inside the car, so don't suggest it to kids who are prone to carsickness!

The It person picks out something in the car (or wherever you're playing) and says, "I spy something with my little eye and the color of it is..." and says what color the object is.

Each person takes a turn guessing which object the person is thinking of.

The person who guesses the object gets to be It next. You can also take turns being It to make sure that everyone gets a chance to be It.

License Plate 🚗 Game

Each person picks a different multiple of 10 less than 100; for example, they may pick 00, 10, 20, etc.

When the game starts, everyone looks for license plates with his or her selected number on them. When someone spots a plate with his number, he calls it out and looks for the next number in sequence.

The first one to get to the next multiple of 10 (from 20 to 30, for example) wins.

20 Questions

One person thinks of a Person, Place or Thing and tells everyone in which of these categories it belongs.

The rest of the players take turns asking the It person yes/no questions in order to figure out what the person, place or thing is. However, the players are allowed only 20 questions to figure out what the It person is thinking of. The It person keeps count of how many questions have been asked.

If the other players haven't guessed correctly within twenty questions, the It person reveals what the person, place or thing was — and is It again. However, if somebody guesses correctly, he is It the next time.

Bizz-Buzz

This game will get everyone's head in a knot; it requires a great deal of concentration. It is also a game of speed; anyone who thinks for more than a few seconds loses.

The first person will say, "One" and each person will count off clockwise from the first person.

However, any number that has a five in it (5, 15, 25) or is a multiple of five (5, 10, 20) must be replaced by "Bizz." Any number that has a seven in it or is a multiple of seven is replaced by "Buzz." Any number that has both a five or seven in it (57, 75), or is a multiple of both (35, 70), is replaced with "Bizz-Buzz."

When someone makes a mistake, that player is out. The last person left is the winner.

To make the game easier, start with just the Bizz and add the Buzz once everyone's got the swing of things. To make it harder, use three instead of five for Bizz and/or switch directions on every Bizz-Buzz.

As with many of these games, the kids may not care about losers and winners; when someone makes a mistake, just start over with the next person and nobody is out.

GHOST

Ghost also requires concentration — and that the participants are capable spellers.

The first person says a letter, such as "B". The next person adds another letter, such as "A", to form "BA". Each person in turn adds another letter that can be used to spell a real word, but the trick is not to actually spell a complete word. So, for example, if the letters spell "BAL", the next person must be careful not to say "L" since "BALL" is a complete word. She may say "A", however, which could be used to spell "BALANCE", or "O" to spell "BALONEY".

If the person spells a complete word — even if it's by accident (she may have been thinking of BALLET) — then she is assigned a "G" for G-H-O-S-T. For each mistake, she's assigned another letter in GHOST. When she gets the T, she's out of the game. The winner is the last person left.

If a person does not believe that a word can be made from the existing letters, she may challenge the person who said the last letter. If he can think of a word, the challenger gets a letter in GHOST; if not, then he gets a letter.

The Alphabet

a b c d e f g h i j k l m n o p q r s t u v w x y z

Game

The object of this game is to find each letter of the alphabet in sequence by looking at signs, license plates, passing blimps, wherever they might occur. When a player sees a letter, she calls it out and points to it. Only the person who calls it out first gets to use it.

The first person to get from A to Z wins.

Categories

The first person names a category such as Animals, Types of Cars, Things in a Kitchen, People Who Wear Uniforms, etc. Going clockwise, each player names an item in that category until someone is not able to think of one. That person is out, and the next person in the circle starts the next category.

The game repeats until one person is left, and that person is the winner. You may also choose to simply restart the game each time, without anyone going out.

When playing with bigger kids, you can play that each person has to name an item from the category whose name starts with the last letter of the item given by the previous player. For example, the category might be Things on a Camping Trip, and if the first person says "flashlight" the next person must name a thing typically found on a camping trip that begins with the letter "T", such as "tent".

Mini-Mysteries

The trick to this game is to come up with the crime scenes (or brain teasers); the ones below are just a start.

This game is very similar to 20 Questions except that the players are trying to solve a mystery. You describe a crime scene, and the other players have 20 yes/no questions with which to try to guess what happened.

Here are some sample scenes:

Scene 1: *A man is lying dead in the middle of the desert, with a backpack on. There are no footsteps in the sand around him. How did he die?*
Answer: *He was parachuting and his parachute failed to open.*

Scene 2: *A man is hanging from a ceiling beam with nothing but a puddle under him. How did he hang himself?*
Answer: *He stood on a block of ice.*

Scene 3: *John and Mary are lying dead in a pool of water and the cat is on the mantel smiling. What has happened?*
Answer: *John and Mary are fish, and the cat knocked their fish bowl off the mantel.*

Scene 4: *After a forest fire, a man is found dead in a tree, wearing a scuba suit. How did he get there?*
Answer: *He was scuba diving when a helicopter lifted him out of the ocean in a bucket of water that was used to douse the fire.*

Scene 5 (most difficult!): *A man is lying dead on the ground, surrounded by 106 bicycles. What happened?*
Answer: *He was playing poker using bicycle cards. There are 52 cards in a deck, each with two bicycles on it. 106 bicycles would indicate 53 cards; the dead man must've brought an extra ace to the game and the other players found out and killed him.*

Th🖐mb Wrestling

These last two games are last-ditch efforts to pass the time — but they work pretty much anytime and anywhere: in the car, on the sidelines, in line at the grocery store.

Two players hook the four fingers of their right hands together, with their thumbs pointing up.

Each player touches her thumb down alternately on top of her and her opponent's fists, saying, "One, two, three, four. I declare a thumb war." Then each player attempts to pin the other's thumb down with her thumb for three seconds; the player who succeeds wins.

Under-Over

Two players face each other, one with her hands held out in front of her, flat with the palms up; the other with his hands palms down and just above the first player's hands.

The first player tries to flip her hands over to slap the top of the second player's hands before the second player can pull his hands away. This is repeated until the first player is successful in slapping the top of the second player's hands, at which point the players switch hand positions so that the second player's hands are now face-up on the bottom.

Whiteboard Games

Save a tree; buy a whiteboard! You can get a small easel or laptop whiteboard, which is more fun for the kids and much less wasteful than paper.

If the kids aren't prone to carsickness, these are also good games for the car.

Hangman

One person — the hangman — draws a scaffold (an upside down "L" will do the trick) and thinks of a word. She then draws a blank for each letter in the word, next to the scaffold.

The other players take turns guessing letters. If the letter is in the word, the hangman writes the letter into the correct blank. If the letter is not in the word, the hangman writes the letter off to the side and draws the head of a stick figure hanging from the scaffold. For each wrong guess, the hangman draws another part of the stick figure. The parts typically include the head, a torso, two legs and two arms.

The game is over when a player guesses the word, in which case he becomes the hangman. It also ends if the hangman draws the whole man before anyone has guessed the word, in which case she is the hangman again.

Proper nouns are not allowed, unless you agree upon special categories of words.

Especially with little kids, you may want to add hands and feet to the hangman; maybe a mouth and eyes...a nose...

Tic Tac Toe

This game probably doesn't need any explanation.

Draw two perpendicular sets of parallel lines. Each person is designated as X's or O's.

Each person takes turns drawing an X or an O into an empty box. The first one to get three X's or O's in a row (up-and-down, across or diagonally) wins.

Dots and Lines

There's more strategy to this game than you might think; players are often caught by surprise toward the end.

Make a grid of dots, at least 10 dots by 10 dots.

Each player takes turns drawing a line between any two consecutive dots (vertical and horizontal only, no diagonals). However, if a player is able to complete a square — or two squares — by drawing a line, he puts his initials inside of the square(s) and gets to draw another line. The player keeps going until his line fails to make a square.

The game is over when all of the dots have been connected into squares.

The winner is the person whose initials appear in the most boxes.

Jotto

Jotto is played by two people and requires paper and pen for each.

Each person thinks of a five-letter word — his "secret word" — and writes it at the top of his sheet of paper. The players then take turns trying to figure out the other person's word.

On each player's turn, the player will say a five-letter word. The other player responds with the number of letters that the guessed word shares with her secret word. The order of the letters in the word doesn't matter.

The players take turns figuring out what letters are in the other person's word and then arranging them into real words and guessing those words until they guess the correct word.

Always spell out words as they are guessed in order to avoid any confusion.

To figure out which letters in a word match the secret word, use a process of elimination. For example, if a player guesses "steal" and the other player responds that one or more letters match her secret word, the first player might guess "stall" the next time. If there is one less matching letter, then the secret word must contain an "E".

Agree in advance whether the secret words may include the same letter more than once. Repeating letters makes the game more challenging.

CARD Games

ere's a tip: Some toddlers will play with a deck of cards endlessly and will want to play with yours. Try to have a throw-away deck for them to entertain themselves with, but only give them a portion of it in order to minimize the clean-up afterwards.

In all of these games, a helpful rule to remember is the following: A card laid is a card played. You can't pick up a card that you've just played in order to play a different one.

Unless otherwise indicated, all of these games may be played with two or more people. When a game calls for dealing out the entire deck of cards, there may be some extra cards, depending upon the number of players. Just continue to deal the cards out, giving some players an extra card.

Old Maid

This game is very, very easy to play, which is why many of us will remember it as being the first card game that we played. It requires at least three people.

The goal of this game is not to be left with only the "Old Maid" in your hand.

The dealer takes all of the queens except for the queen of spades — the Old Maid — out of a deck of cards and deals the rest of the cards to the players. Each person discards any pairs in her hand and arranges her hand so that only she can see the cards in it.

The person to the left of the dealer picks a card from the dealer's hand. If it makes a pair with another card in his hand, he discards the pair. Then the person to his left picks a card from his deck, and play continues until one person is left with only the Old Maid.

Go Fish

The dealer deals five cards to each player (seven cards if you only have two players). The rest of the deck is placed face-down in the middle of the table. All of the players arrange their cards in their hands so that only they may see them.

Each player, starting from the left of the dealer and going clock-wise, asks any other player for a specific number or face card (jack, queen, king). If the second player has one or more of the requested cards in her hand, she gives them to the person who requested them and the first person gets to go again and asks another player for some cards.

If a player does not have the requested cards, she says, "Go Fish." The first player takes a card from the deck. If it is the number or face card that he requested, he shows it and goes again; otherwise, his turn is over.

When a player ends up with all four of a number (such as all four aces), he puts them to the side, as a "book." The goal is to have the most books at the end of the game.

The game continues until one player has no cards left in his hand. If all of the players still have cards in their hands but there are no cards in the middle, play still continues without picking.

Note that the winner may not be the first person to get rid of all his cards!

To make this game easier for little kids, you can play with pairs instead of books.

This game is still pretty easy for young kids; there's not much strategy involved.

The dealer deals seven cards to each player, puts the deck face-down in the center and flips the top card over so that it is face-up next to the deck.

The person to the dealer's left must play a card of the same suit or value as the center card (for example, if the center card is a 6 of hearts, the player must discard a heart or a 6 of another suit). If she doesn't have such a card, she must pick from the deck until she has a card that she can play.

However, if the person has an 8 — or picks one from the pile — she can play that on the pile and say what suit the next person must play. Obviously, she'll want to call the suit for which she has the most cards in her hand.

The next person going clockwise plays, either matching the number or suit that was played or, if a "crazy eight" was played, the suit called by the person who played it.

The first person to get rid of all of her cards wins.

Be prepared: War can last a long time.

For War, deal all of the cards to the players. Each player puts his cards into a face-down pile on the table or may hold them in their hand.

On each turn, all of the players flip over the top card on their piles into the center. Whoever has the highest card (2's are lowest and aces are highest) takes all of the cards played on that turn.

If two or more people tie for the highest card, they "play war". To play war, each person who is part of the tie lays down three cards face-down and one card face-up. As they do this, they say, "1-2-3 means war!"

Whoever has the highest new card takes all of the cards. If there is still a tie, the people who are part of the tie play war again until one person wins.

When a person runs out of cards, he's out of the game. The game ends when one player has all the cards. That person is the winner.

Slap Jack

SlapJack is similar to War but requires attention and speed rather than luck.

Like War, deal the whole deck out to all of the players. Each player must put her deck face-down in front of her.

Starting to the dealer's left, each player flips one card from her deck face-up into the center. She should be sure to flip it forward quickly so that she can't see it before the other players, nor they before her.

If a player flips a jack into the center, all of the players try to slap the card. The player who gets her hand on the jack first wins, and places all the cards in the center pile at the bottom of her pile.

The game continues until one player has all of the cards. You should decide whether somebody who loses all of her cards may continue to try to slap jacks so that she can get back into the game.

This game is a bit more difficult, mostly because of how many moves can be made in a turn, and because there is some strategy involved. Consequently, that makes it more fun for the bigger kids and adults.

The dealer deals seven cards to each player; the rest of the deck is placed face-down in the middle. Flip over four cards from the deck so that they are face-up and arranged around the deck, one on each side, pointing away from the deck. These are the "foundation piles".

The person to the left of the dealer goes first. This person picks a card from the pile and then may make a number of moves. The valid moves are as follows:

▌ Place a king in a corner– face-up and pointing away from a corner of the deck — to create a new foundation pile. The king can come from your hand or from one of the foundation piles.

▌ Play a card from your hand onto a foundation pile. The card must be the opposite color and one less in value than the card on the foundation pile. For example, only a red jack may be played on top of a black queen. Aces are the lowest card, so nothing can be played on an ace. Play the cards extending out in a line so that you can see all of the cards in a pile.

▌ Move an entire foundation pile onto another foundation pile if the top card of the second pile is the opposite color and one less in value than the bottom card in the first pile. So, a pile that has a black 7 at the top can be placed on a pile that has a red 8 on the bottom.

▌ If one of the four original foundation piles is moved so that there is no pile in that position, you can play any card from your hand into that position. If possible, you'll want to play a card that will allow you to play as many cards as possible in your hand. For example, you might play a red 8 if you also have a black 7 in your hand, allowing you to play both cards.

A player can make any number of these moves in one turn. For example, she may move a foundation pile onto a king in the corner, play the red 8 and black 7 from her hand into the new foundation pile, move another foundation pile that starts with a red 6 onto the new pile — and thus free up another foundation pile to play on.

If the player can't make any moves, she passes and the player to her left takes a turn.

The winner is the first person to play all the cards in her hand. If nobody has won and the center pile is gone, continue playing until somebody wins. If nobody is able to play at the end, the game is a draw.

S♥P♠E♣E♦D

Older kids enjoy this game because it is all about speed. It is sometimes known as "Spit".

This game is for only two players, and the goal is to get rid of all of your cards as fast as possible.

The dealer deals the whole deck out to the two players. Each player makes five face-down piles ("stockpiles") next to each other; the first pile to the left has one card, the pile to the right of that has two cards, the pile to the right of that has three cards and so forth. Turn the top card over on each pile.

Each player must hold the remainder of her cards in a deck in one hand. These decks are the "spit cards" or "spit decks."

When both players are ready, they call, "1-2-3 Spit!" and each flips the top card from her spit deck into the middle, between the two rows of stockpiles. These cards become the "spit piles".

At this point, the players play as fast as they can since they want to be the first to get rid of all of their cards. Using only their free hands, the players can make the following moves:

▎Play one of the face-up cards on her stockpiles onto a spit pile. In order to do this, the card has to have a value one more or less than the spit pile card (for example, if the spit pile has a 4 on top, she can play a 3 or a 5). She can also play kings on aces and vice versa. When she plays a card off one of her stockpiles, she turns over the next card in the stockpile.

▎If she plays all the cards in one of her stockpiles, she can move a face-up card from another stockpile onto where the first stockpile used to be, allowing her to turn over another card on the second stockpile.

The idea is to play as fast you can so that you can take advantage of the spit piles. If a 3 is on top, you want to be sure to play your 2 or 4 before the other person does. At the same time, you might want to keep an eye on the other person's piles so that you don't help them; for example, you might want to play the 2 instead of the 4 if you see that your opponent has a 5 on one of his piles.

If the players stop because nobody can play, both shout, "1-2-3 Spit!" again and each plays the top card from her spit deck onto her spit pile and continues play. If a player doesn't have any spit cards, the other player will still play her spit card to continue play.

When either player gets rid of all of her stockpiles but still has spit cards, or both players are unable to play and have run out of spit cards, the person with the fewest cards selects the smallest spit pile. She may not touch or count the cards to determine which is the smaller pile. Optionally, you can play that either player may slap the smallest pile to claim it as soon as one player gets rid of her stockpiles.

Each player combines the cards in her deck, stockpiles and spit pile and shuffles them. The players lay the cards out in piles as they did at the start, and play continues as described above.

If a player has fewer than 15 cards, she deals her cards into as many stockpiles as she can but will not have any spit cards. In this case, there will be only one spit pile, and the first one to get rid of her stockpiles does NOT take the spit pile. The other person will combine the spit pile with the rest of her cards, and both will shuffle and re-deal their layout.

The first to get rid of all of her cards wins the game.

SPIT

Spit is an easier version of Speed — but is still all about speed. More than two people may play this game.

Each player has his own deck of well-shuffled cards. Make sure that the decks have different designs on them so that they can be easily separated. Each player lays out the top four cards in his deck face-up side-by-side in front of him. He holds the remainder of his deck face-down in one hand.

All of the players say, "1-2-3 Spit!" at the same time and then play the top card from the decks in their hands face-up into the center. Then each person, using only his free hand, moves the cards in front of him onto any of the piles in the center. Cards are played by number; they must be one more or less in value than the top card in the pile. For example, only a 2 or 4 may be played on a 3. Aces can be played on kings and vice versa.

When a player plays one of his four cards, he flips another one off of the deck in his hand face-up into the empty space.

When all of the players are stuck and can't play, they say, "1-2-3 Spit!" and flip new cards into the center, on top of the original piles.

Play continues until one person gets rid of his cards; that person is the winner. If all players are stuck and have no more cards in their hands with which to "spit", the one with the fewest cards wins.

You can also play with a single deck for a shorter game.

Concentration

Lay out all of the cards face-down; they can be in neat lines or spread around randomly.

Each player takes a turn by turning over two cards. If he gets a matched pair, he keeps the pair and goes again. If not, he turns the cards back over and the next person takes a turn. Continue play until all of the cards are gone.

The trick is obviously to remember which cards have been turned over and where they are so that you can find them later, when you turn over a matching card.

The person with the most pairs wins.

For smaller kids, you can use just part of the deck, making sure to pull out all four suits of each number that you use.

Spoons

The dealer arranges spoons — one less than there are players — in a circle in the center of the table or floor, and deals four cards to each player. The dealer places the rest of the deck to his right. Each person picks up his cards and arranges them so that only he can see them.

The dealer picks up one card at a time from the deck on his right and discards one card face-down to his left so that the player to his left can pick up the cards and do the same thing. The goal is to get all four cards of the same number as the cards are passed around (keeping in mind that a player must never have more than four cards in her hands).

When a player gets four of a kind, he carefully pulls a spoon off the table so that nobody will notice. However, if someone else sees him steal the spoon, or notices that one is missing, she may also pull a spoon off the table, whether or not she has four of a kind.

The person who does not get a spoon is the loser and must sit out for the rest of the game.

The person to the left of the dealer deals and starts the game over, using one less spoon.

The winner is the last person to have a spoon after all the other players lose.

The cards may go around the circle several times before someone gets four of a kind.

The dealer helps to set the speed of the game. Other players may slow it down but the faster, the crazier!

A more difficult but funnier version of this game is "Tongues," in which you stick out your tongue — instead of stealing a spoon — when you get four of a kind.

I Doubt It!

Kids get a kick out of this game because it essentially condones cheating. It requires at least three players.

The dealer deals all of the cards to the players. Each person arranges the cards in his or her hand so that only he/she can see them.

The person to the left of the dealer starts and plays all of the aces in his hand, saying how many he played, such as, "One ace." The next person going clockwise lays down one or more twos and says how many she played, and so on. However, if a player does not have the correct cards, she may play any other card(s) while claiming to play the correct ones.

If someone doubts that a player has played what she claims, the doubter says, "I doubt it!" The doubter turns over the card(s) that were just played. If the doubter is correct, the cheater must take all of the cards in the pile; otherwise the doubter must take all of the cards. Play then continues.

The player who gets rid of all of his cards first wins.

This game can also be played with only one card discarded at a time. This takes longer but is more challenging since, in the other version, people quickly end up with all four of a kind so that it's very hard to lie.

You may also play that the person who successfully challenges someone else may call and start play with a new number.

Decide ahead of time whether or not real cheating is allowed — such as hiding cards, playing more than are called, etc. This version is also known by other names, including at least one unprintable but very common name!

DOUBLE DOUBLE

There are many different types of solitaire; don't forget to teach them to the kids. Solitaire will keep the kids busy and thinking when you need a little quiet time.

Double Solitaire is a version that can be played by two or more players and is all about speed. It requires one deck of cards per player; the decks should have different designs on the back so that they can be easily separated.

Double Solitaire is the same as Klondike, which is one of the most popular Solitaire games, except that two or more people play at the same time.

Each player makes seven piles in a row in front of them, with only the top card face-up on each pile. The first pile to the left has one card, the second has two cards and so forth. The players hold the remainder of the cards face-down in their hands.

Make room between the two players' piles for four foundation piles per player.

The players start by saying, "On your mark! Get set! Go!" and then play as fast as they can in hopes of being the one to play the most cards into the middle.

A player may move a face-up card — or pile of face-up cards — from one of his piles to another face-up card if the cards will be in descending numerical and alternating color order (for example, a red

SOLITAIRE SOLITAIRE

4 may be played on a black 5). Whenever the face-up card(s) on a pile is moved, the next card in the pile is turned over. If the last card in a pile has been moved, a king may be placed into the blank spot.

In addition, cards may be played into the center, onto foundation piles. As aces turn up, the players will place them in the middle and may play on them in increasing numerical sequence of the same suit (the 2 of diamonds may be played only on the ace of diamonds).

Players must call out the number and suit of the cards as they play them on the foundation piles.

Each player may play on any of the foundation piles, no matter who played the original ace in the pile.

When a player cannot play onto any of his personal piles or the foundation piles, he turns over the cards in his deck (one-by-one or, to make it a little more challenging, three-by-three) and may play them onto any of the piles. He keeps turning over the cards until he goes through the whole deck without playing a card. However, his opponent may play a card on a foundation pile that will allow him to play a card and thus continue play.

The first player to get rid of all of his cards wins. If both players still have cards but neither can play, then the player who played the most cards wins.

Hearts

People of all ages enjoy playing Hearts. It's a classic game for family gatherings. You must have three people to play, but may want to limit the number of players to five or six.

The dealer deals out all of the cards. Any extra cards are placed in the center of the table. Each person looks at his cards and arranges them in his hand as he sees fit.

The goal of the game is to have the least points at the end. The scoring is as follows:

▌ Each heart is worth one point.

▌ The queen of spades is worth 13 points

▌ The jack of diamonds is worth minus 10 points.

Consequently, players want to have the jack of diamonds at the end of the game, but not any hearts or the queen of spades.

The person to the left of the dealer plays a card into the center of the table and everyone else plays in order around the circle until each person has played one card. The players are required to play a card of the same suit as what was led (the card played by the first person). The person who plays the highest card of that suit wins the trick (all of the played cards), puts it face-down in front of him and leads the next trick. Aces are the highest card of a suit.

If during a trick a player does not have any cards of the suit that was led, he may play any other card in his hand. For example, he may play a heart or the queen of spades in order to give points to the person who takes the trick. If he doesn't have the queen of spades, he may instead play the king or ace of spades to help ensure that he won't win a spade trick later that includes the queen of spades.

If cards were dealt into the center, the first trick will take them. The person who wins the first trick shows the cards to everyone else and places them with the rest of the trick face-down in front of him.

No one may pick up the face-down cards to see what has been played since remembering what has been played is an important aspect to the game.

Once all of the cards have been played, the tricks in front of each person are totaled up to determine how many points each person has. Typically, a game of Hearts will last until everyone has dealt at least one hand. The person with the lowest total across all hands is the winner.

An easier but less exciting way to play the game is not to assign the jack of diamonds any negative points. Then the goal of the game is to avoid winning any tricks in order to avoid gaining any points. When playing with the jack of diamonds, quite a bit more strategy is required since then you want to win at least one trick.

Typically, players are allowed to "shoot the moon". Shooting the moon requires that a single player get all of the hearts, the queen of spades and the jack of diamonds. If the player is successful, he wins negative 100 points. Players will try to do this when they have a very good hand (lots of high cards) or are close to losing the game anyhow!

Another common rule is for each player to pass three cards from his hand to the person on his left after the dealer has dealt the cards. What a player chooses to pass depends upon his strategy for winning that hand.

Card and Magic Tricks

Kids about six and up enjoy these tricks. Even adults are stumped as to how they work, yet they're very easy to perform. The kids will want to try them out on everyone.

Only a few tricks are included here; the budding magician can find many more in the library or online.

Going to the Show ▪▪▪

There is actually no trick to this card trick — the audience can see everything that you do, and the cards will simply work out if you follow the steps properly.

Pull all of the face cards and aces out of the deck and put the deck to the side; you won't use it anymore. Sort the cards so that all of the aces are on top (face-down), followed by the kings, the queens and the jacks. It's okay for your audience to see you do these things.

Flip each of the top cards — the aces — face-up into four separate piles. While you do this, you tell the audience that the Ace family has gone to a show.

Flip the next four cards from the deck — the kings this time — face-up on top of the aces so that the aces and kings are exposed, while saying that the King family has also gone to the show and are chatting with the Ace family in the lobby.

Repeat with the queens and the jacks, elaborating on the story as much as you want.

While saying, "The show is about to begin, so it's time for each family to go to its seats," flip each pile over and put the first pile on top of the second pile, that pile on top of the third pile and that pile on top of the last pile so that a single pile is on the table.

Tell someone in the audience to cut the cards by taking part of the pile and setting it down on the table and then putting the remaining cards on top; do this a few times.

Pick up the deck and lay the cards one-by-one into four face-down piles, saying, "The usher is showing them to their seats."

Turn the decks over and fan them out, saying, "And, as you can see, all of the families are sitting together!"

All of the aces will be in one pile, the kings in another, and so on.

Bury the Aces

This trick will really stump the audiences but, like the previous one, there's really no trick involved. You just need to be sure to follow the directions carefully.

Pull the four aces out into a pile; the audience may see you do this.

Deal the remaining cards one-by-one into three face-down piles. Do this until there are 14 cards in the first (left-most) pile and 15 in each of the second and third piles. This will leave four cards, which you'll put down in a fourth pile.

Tell the audience that you — with their help — will bury the aces into the deck of cards.

Put one of the aces face-down on top of the first pile. Ask the helper to put as many cards from the second pile as she chooses on top of the ace on the first pile.

Put an ace face-down on the second pile and have the helper place a portion of the third pile on top of the second ace.

Put an ace face-down on the third pile and have the helper put the fourth pile on top of this one. This leaves three piles and one ace.

Take the third (rightmost) pile and put it on top of the second pile and put that pile on top of the first pile. This leaves one pile and the last ace.

Deal all of the cards in the one pile into two piles, one by one, starting from the left.

Pick up the left pile and place the top card of that pile on the right pile, and the next card where the first pile was. Deal out the rest of the deck into the two piles.

Continue doing this until only three cards are left in the first pile. Put these three cards on top of the last ace and turn over all four cards as you say, "You buried the aces, but I found them!"

126

Aces on TOP

Have the kids practice this one on you a few times before they perform it for anyone else; they often confuse themselves the first few times through. And tell them not to introduce this trick by name since that gives away the ending!

Out of view of your audience, pull the four aces out of the deck and place them face-down on top of the deck. Shuffle the deck in front of the audience, being careful to keep the four aces on top.

Put the deck face-down on the table and ask an audience member to create four piles by moving the cards around per your instructions.

For example, ask your helper to:

▌ Move approximately half of the cards from the pile (pile 1) into a new pile (pile 2).

▌ Move half of the cards from pile 1 to a new pile (pile 3).

▌ Move two cards from pile 2 to pile 3.

▌ Move half of the cards from pile 2 to a new pile (pile 4).

▌ Move half of the cards in pile 3 to pile 2.

▌ Move one card from pile 4 to pile 1.

▌ Move one card from pile 2 to pile 3.

Ask your helper to turn over the top card on each pile. Your audience will be surprised to see an ace on each one.

Be creative moving the cards around in order to really surprise the audience — just don't forget where the aces are!

White Magic

Tell your audience that you can read their minds; that you will leave the room and that while you're gone, they'll select an object — and that you'll be able to identify it without any clues when you re-enter the room.

Your assistant will stay in the room while you step out. When you return, ask everyone to think about the selected object. Your assistant will point out various objects in the room, asking whether each one is the selected object, to which you'll respond, "No." However, when the assistant points out a white object, you'll know that the next object will be the selected object, at which point you'll say, "That's it."

Play several times, varying the color or using another clue in order to keep your audience guessing!

Musical Games

129

Musical Chairs

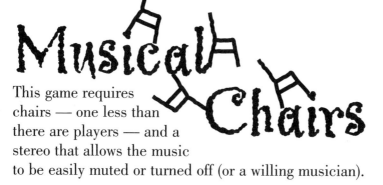

This game requires chairs — one less than there are players — and a stereo that allows the music to be easily muted or turned off (or a willing musician).

One person must be in charge of the music — the DJ — and does not play.

The chairs are lined up in a row, facing outward in alternating directions. The DJ starts the music and leaves it on for some part of a minute while the players circle around the chairs. When he turns it off, each of the players must sit in a chair. Since there is one less chair than players, one player will not have a chair. That person is out for the rest of the game.

The DJ takes a chair out of the line and restarts the music. The game is repeated until only one person — the winner — is left.

Freeze Dance

Freeze Dance is similar to Musical Chairs, with a DJ starting and stopping the music. It will generate giggles as the kids try to hold their sometimes-silly positions. This is a classic for sleepover parties.

For this game, the DJ starts the music and the kids start dancing, the sillier the better. When the music stops, the players must freeze. If the DJ sees anyone moving, that person is out.

Continue until one person is left; that person is the winner.

Limbo

This dance is always a big hit with the younger kids at wedding receptions, if you can find a broom or mop or other stick. Any music will do.

Two people hold the broom at opposite ends at about shoulder-level of the tallest dancer. All of the dancers line up behind the first dancer, who is facing the broom. Each dancer dances facing forward toward the broom, but when he gets to the broom, he must bend over backward so that his head is the last thing to go under the broom (he may not duck his head forward). Once he goes under the broom, he dances his way to the back of the line.

When all of the dancers have gone under the broom, the people holding it lower it a couple of inches, and thus the limbo continues.

If a dancer fails to go under the broom properly, or touches it or falls, he's out. The last player left is the winner.

If the kids are all younger, they probably won't care about winning and may have a bit of trouble doing the limbo properly — it's probably better to just let them play and not worry about anyone losing or winning. Big kids may be more competitive.

Other Indoor Games

Arts and crafts and baking are other great indoor activities; however, there is a wealth of books that cover these activities exhaustively and creatively, so they are not included here. But don't forget how much kids enjoy those activities on a rainy or snowy day.

You'll sometimes wish you'd never suggested building a fort when your living room or dining room ends up in complete disarray. But if you've got a room and patience that will withstand the disarray, the kids love building and playing in forts. Be sure to require the kids to return everything to its proper place once they've tired of the game.

There are no particular rules to building forts; the goal is usually to create a confined space that completely shuts out the outside world. You can hang blankets off of the dining room table and layer the floor with pillows and cushions; you can drape sheets between beds or between the back of the couch and several chairs.

As is often the case, you're limited only by your imagination.

Charades For BIG Kids

This version of charades is a timeless source of fun for big kids and adults. Not everyone likes to play, but those who do usually can't be stopped.

You'll need strips of paper, a pen or pencil, a stopwatch and two hats (or baskets or brown bags).

Divide into two teams.

Each team writes the titles of movies, books, sayings, songs, plays and/or TV shows on pieces of paper, puts them into a hat and gives the hat to the opposite team.

A person from one team selects a piece of paper from her team's hat and then pantomimes the title written on the piece of paper; no verbal cues are allowed. Her team has two minutes to guess the title. The team scores a point if she succeeds.

The other team then takes a turn, and so forth until all players have acted out a charade. The team with the most points wins.

You should decide ahead of time how many rounds you'd like to play, but this game is often extended "just one more round" once everyone starts getting into it. You may also choose to allow more time to guess the title.

There are some standard rules for what is allowed when a person is pantomiming a title. Everyone should agree on the rules before starting. Following are the rules — or tips — that are generally accepted for giving hints.

Type of title:
Book: Put your palms together and open them, as though opening a book.

Movie: To imitate a projector, hold one hand up to your eye in an "O" shape and use the other hand to pretend to crank a handle next to it.

TV Show: Draw a square in the air to indicate a TV screen.

Song: Pretend to sing.

Play: Pretend to pull a cord, as though pulling open the playhouse curtains.

Number of words in the title:
Hold up a number of fingers equal to the number of words in the title. To indicate a particular word in the title, hold up the number of fingers representing its placement in the title (for example, two fingers for the second word in the title).

Number of syllables in each word:
Lay a number of fingers equal to the number of syllables in the word on your forearm.

If you are acting out just a single syllable, lay the finger down representing that syllable on your forearm.

Other hints:
Little word: Hold your thumb and forefinger close together to indicate a short word.

Big word: Hold your thumb and forefinger far apart.

Longer word: Move your hands apart, as though to stretch the word that somebody has just guessed. This is helpful if, for example, somebody says "fridge" and the word is "refrigerator," or "hide" and the word is "hiding."

Shorter word: Make a chopping motion.

Sounds like: Cup your hand to your ear before you act out something that sounds like the word you are trying to get your team to guess.

Keep guessing: Wave your hand toward you to indicate "come on, keep guessing, you're close!"

You guessed it: Point to your nose. You can use this with the "longer word" or "shorter word" clue to make sure they know which word they are shortening or elongating. Obviously, if they've guessed the whole title, you can tell them so.

Charades For Little Kids

This version of charades eliminates all of the rules of the adult version that would likely be too challenging for the younger kids.

Also, instead of movie and book titles, use activities ("playing soccer," "putting on my pajamas," "riding a pony"), animals and cartoon characters. You can use very simple and familiar books and movies, such as "Sleeping Beauty" and "Little Red Riding Hood," but you may still need to give the kids hints to act them out.

You'll need strips of paper, a pen or pencil and a hat (or basket or brown paper bag).

Write the names of activities and animals on pieces of paper and put them into a hat. The first child will select one of the pieces of paper out of the hat and act out the charade while the other children guess. You can put a time limit on each turn if you want to.

The person who correctly guesses the activity gets to go the next time — or you can keep score of who guesses the most correct answers while letting each child take a turn being the actor. Younger kids generally don't seem too interested in who's winning or losing as much as they are in their turn to act out the charade.

Dictionary

Dictionary is a game for the older kids. Players need to be able to come up with definitions that sound like they're straight out of the dictionary. The game can be hilarious; the most serious-sounding definitions are sometimes the funniest.

You'll need a dictionary, lots of small slips of paper and a pen or pencil for each person.

The It person will look up a word in the dictionary and make sure that nobody in the room has heard of it before. Each person makes up a definition for the word, writes it on a slip of paper and puts the slip of paper into the hat. You may set a time limit if you think it necessary. During this time, the It person will write down the true definition and slip that into the hat as well.

The It person reads all of the definitions, including the real one, in random order. The rest of the players vote for which definition they think is the real one. After everyone has voted, the It person reveals who wrote which definition.

A person gets a point if she guesses correctly or if anyone else thought that her definition was the correct one. The It person gets a point for each person who guesses the correct definition.

Each person takes a turn selecting a word, and the winner is the person with the most points when the game ends.

Paper Football

This game can help pass the time in a doctor's office or restaurant or anywhere else that has a flat surface.

To make a paper football, cut a strip from an 8.5 x 11-inch piece of paper lengthwise (the wider the strip, the bigger the football) and fold the bottom corner up to form a triangle. Keep folding the strip into a triangle until you run out of paper, and tuck the remainder into the "ball".

Lay the football down so that it hangs off of the edge of the table in front of one player. That player will push the football down the table toward the other player by bumping the palm of his hand against the end of the table and ball. The second player will push it back by giving it a flick with the back of his fingertips. The first player flicks it back. This continues until the ball partially hangs off one side of the table. This is a touchdown for six points for the person who successfully flicked the ball to the edge.

If the ball goes off the table at any point, the player whose side it is on will put it back on the edge of the table and restart play.

The player who scores a touchdown takes the football and stands it on one point on her end of the table, with a fingertip on the top point and the third point directed toward her. The ball should be leaning back somewhat. Her opponent will create a goal at the other end by resting his wrists on the edge of the table and forming his thumbs and index fingers into upright L's joined at the thumbs. The scorer will attempt to put the ball through the goal by flicking its lower edge. A point is awarded for making it through the goal.

The other person places the football back on the edge of the table and puts it back into play.

Penny Football

Should you not have any paper available, you can also play football with three coins on a table.

The first player places three coins on the table, with the center one at the edge of the table and the other two further out, in an inverted pyramid.

The player slides the back coin between the other two coins by flicking it with his fingertips. He continues to flick the furthest back coin between the other two until he scores a touchdown by flicking the coin into a goal. The goal is made by the opponent's hand; she lays the pinkie and index finger of one hand flat onto the table, with her knuckles behind the edge of the table.

If the flicked coin doesn't go all the way through the invisible line drawn by the other coins, hits another coin, or goes off the table, the other person gets the "ball" and restarts the play from her side of the table.

To get an extra point after scoring a touchdown, the player spins the coin on its edge on the table by putting a finger on the top edge and flicking it with his index finger on his other hand. He must catch the coin by pinching it between his thumbs before it falls. He puts his knuckles down on the table wherever he caught the coin, brings the coin back between his thumbs and flicks it over a goalpost made by the opponent's hands as described for paper football. If he does not catch the quarter with his thumbs, or misses the goal, he does not score the extra point.

Cootie Catchers

Cootie Catchers might fall into the category of arts-and-crafts, but they're childhood classics and easy to make. Despite their name, these are actually fortune-telling tools.

To make a Cootie Catcher, you'll need an 8.5 x 11-inch piece of paper and a pencil or pen.

First, fold the paper into a big triangle — one short side against one long side — and cut the extra paper off the long side in order to get a perfect square.

Unfold the paper and fold it in half in each direction, just to make it more flexible. Lay it flat and fold each corner of the paper up so that the corners meet in the center.

Flip it over and again fold each corner into the center. Fold it in half in one direction and then unfold it and fold it in the other direction, once again to make it more flexible.

While it's still folded in half, pick it up and slip the thumb and index fingers of each hand into the pockets that have been formed on the bottom of the cootie catcher. Pull all four fingers together to a point so that the top outer edges of the cootie catcher come up together into a point. Open and close your fingers to make the cootie catcher open alternately parallel and perpendicular to yourself.

It's time to put the fortunes on the
cootie catcher. Write the name of a color
on each of the four pockets on the outside
of the cootie catcher, and write a number (1-8)
on each of the triangles on the inside of the
cootie catcher. Lay the cootie catcher flat so that you
can turn up each of the triangles; write a fortune behind
each of the numbers. Fortunes can be a mix of good and bad:
"You'll find a genie in a bottle" or "You'll fall into a toilet."

Put the cootie catcher back onto your thumbs and index fingers and
bring the four corners up to a point. Ask your "customer" to name
one of the colors that are written on the cootie catcher. Spell out
the color, opening the cootie catcher in alternating directions for
each letter.

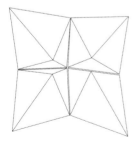

Ask your customer to pick from the numbers
that are showing inside of the cootie catcher.
Count out those numbers, opening the
catcher in alternating directions. Have
your customer pick another number.

Open the cootie catcher to read the fortune
on the back!

At the Dinner Table... or Around the Campfire

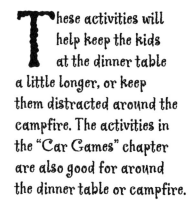

These activities will help keep the kids at the dinner table a little longer, or keep them distracted around the campfire. The activities in the "Car Games" chapter are also good for around the dinner table or campfire.

Master Viking

This game works best with at least five or six players, who are sitting in a circle.

The Master Viking puts his hands up to his head to form horns — he puts the tips of his thumbs on either side of his head and wiggles his fingers. The person to the right of him must pretend to row a boat on her right side; the person to his left must pretend to row a boat to her left.

The Master Viking claps his hands together and points them at any other player (this may be one of the rowers). That person becomes the Master Viking and the people on either side of him must start rowing as appropriate. If anyone misses her cue — doesn't put up her horns or forgets to row on the correct side — she's out of the game.

The last two left are the winners.

Staring Contest

Two people stare at each other until one of them loses by blinking or — more likely — laughing.

Telephone

One person thinks of a phrase and whispers it to the person next to him so that no one else may hear. That person whispers it to the person next to her, and so forth until the last person hears the phrase. The last person says what he heard.

There is no winner, but there is often an entertaining difference between what the first person said and the last person said.

Silly or nonsensical, but syntactically correct, phrases ("I got in trouble when I fell in a puddle with a bottle of beetles.") will make for the most fun. Decide whether players may say "Operator" in order to hear the phrase a second time before passing it on.

Graveyard Face

Everybody must keep a straight face while the It person tries to make them laugh by making funny faces, saying funny things or otherwise being silly.

The winner is the last one to laugh.

Each person takes a turn being It.

Pass the Sentence

One person says a word to start a sentence and, going clockwise, each player adds a word to the sentence.

There is no winner to this game, but silly words and unexpected conjunctions will keep the kids paying attention.

Pass the Story

One person starts a story and at any point in the story, turns it over to the person on his left to continue. Each person makes up another piece of the story and passes it on to the next person.

Pass the Story is a favorite around the campfire. Just be sure to keep in mind the ages of those sitting around the campfire before making the story too scary.

Younger kids may stay enthusiastic longer if you give the storyline an obvious direction at the hand-off. However, be sure not to become possessive about the story; the kids may not take it where you intended, but be sure to go wherever they take it!

Word Fun

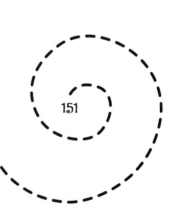

Tongue Twisters

See how quickly you and the kids can say these little tongue twisters:

If Peter Piper picked a peck of pickled peppers,
how many pickled peppers did Peter Piper pick?

She sells shiny seashells by the seashore.

A skunk sat on a stump and thunk the stump stunk,
but the stump thunk the skunk stunk.

How much wood would a woodchuck chuck
if a woodchuck could chuck wood?

The sixth sick sheik's sixth sheep's sick.

Toy boat. Toy boat. Toy boat. Toy boat. Toy boat.

Betty Botter had some butter,
"But," she said, "this butter's bitter.
If I bake this bitter butter,
it would make my batter bitter.
But a bit of better butter,
that would make my batter better."

So she bought a bit of butter,
better than her bitter butter,
and she baked it in her batter,
and the batter was not bitter.
So 'twas better Betty Botter
bought a bit of better butter.

Riddles and Jokes

Since the kids will want to tell these to their friends, have them repeat them back to you after you tell them; otherwise, they usually have a hard time remembering them.

Q: What did one chick say to the other chick when the mama hen laid an orange?
A: Look at the orange mama laid (marmalade).

Q: If Mrs. Sippi gave Miss Souri a New Jersey, what would Delaware?
A: Idaho, Alaska (I don't know, I'll ask her.)

Q: What's black and white and read all over?
A: The newspaper.

Q: Why is 6 afraid of 7?
A: Because 789 (because seven ate nine)

Q: Why can't your nose be 12 inches long?
A: Because then it would be a foot.

Q: Why don't seagulls fly over the bay?
A: Because that would make them bagels (bay gulls).

Q: Why didn't the skeleton cross the road?
A: Because he didn't have any guts.

Q: Why couldn't the skeleton go to the dance?
A: Because he didn't have any body to go with.

Q: Why did the teacher wear sunglasses?
A: Because her students were so bright.

Q: Why did the little boy throw the clock out the window?
A: He wanted to see time fly.

Q: How do you catch a unique monkey?
A: You neak up on him.

Q: What gets wetter and wetter the more it dries?
A: A towel.

Q: A car with no headlights is driving down a road with no street-lights toward a boy wearing black clothes. How does the driver miss the boy?
A: It's daytime.

Q: What kind of ship does Dracula own?
A: A blood vessel.

Q: Why do eggs not tell jokes?
A: Because it cracks them up.

Q: Why did the jelly roll?
A: Because he saw the apple turnover.

Q: Did you hear about the pirate movie?
A: It's rated ARRRRR!

Q: I know your name is (name of other person). How do you spell it?
A: I-T.

Q: What has three feet but no toes?
A: A yard stick.

Q: Why do movie stars stay so cool?
A: Because they have so many fans.

Q: Why should you never tell secrets on a farm?
A: Because the corn has ears and the potatoes have eyes.

Q: There are 5 fish in a bowl and 3 of them drown. How many fish are left?
A: 5 — fish don't drown!!

Q: Why did the boy tip-toe past the medicine cabinet?
A: Because he didn't want to wake up the sleeping pills.

Q: Why did the fish blush?
A: Because it saw the ocean's bottom.

Q: Who's the best dancer at a Halloween party?
A: The Boogie man.

Q: What do you call a cow with no legs?
A: Ground beef.

Q: Where do sick boats go?
A: To the doc(k).

Q: Why does a mummy make a bad birthday gift?
A: It takes too long to unwrap.

Q: What did one strawberry say to the other strawberry?
A: If you'd listened to me, we wouldn't be in this jam.

Q: What did the math book say to the other math book?
A: Gee, I have a lot of problems.

Q: What building has the most stories?
A: The library.

Q: How do you make a tissue dance?
A: Put a little boogie in it.

Q: What did one zombie say to another?
A: Get a life.

Q: Why do they put fences around graveyards?
A: Because everybody is dying to get in.

Q: What did the cat say after the vet finished giving it a shot?
A: Me-OW!!!!

Q: What horse can live in the sea?
A: A seahorse.

Q: What do vampires take when they are sick?
A: Coffin drops.

Q: What do you call two banana peels?
A: A pair of slippers.

Q: What kind of room do you not want to live in?
A: A mushroom.

Q: What do you get when you cross an earthquake with a cow?
A: A milkshake.

Q: Which weighs more: a pound of lead or a pound of feathers?
A: Neither, they both weigh a pound.

Q: What do you call a cow that does not give milk?
A: A milk-dud.

Q: What kind of nails do carpenters hate to hit?
A: Fingernails.

Q: Why do golfers bring an extra pair of socks?
A: In case they get a hole in one.

Q: Where does a ghost live?
A: At the dead end.

Q: What loves peanuts and goes boom, boom, boom?
A: An elephant skipping rope.

Q: Why did the football coach go to the bank?
A: To get his quarter back.

Q: Why did Tigger look in the toilet?
A: He was looking for Pooh.

Q: What did the ocean say to the beach?
A: Nothing. It just waved.

Q: What kind of pet just lies around the house all the time?
A: A carpet.

Q: Where does the general keep his armies?
A: In his sleevies.

Q: Why did the dog lie in the sun?
A: Because he wanted to be a hot dog.

Q: Which animal doesn't play fair?
A: The cheetah.

Q: What do you call a sleeping bull?
A: A bulldozer.

Q: What did the chef name his son?
A: Stew.

Q: Where does a mouse live?
A: In a mouse house.

Q: What do you call a kid's bicycle?
A: A tyke bike.

Knock-knock Jokes

Like the riddles, have the kids repeat these to you in order to help them better remember them for sharing with their friends.

Knock-knock jokes are a dialogue between two people. One person knows the joke, which is usually a play on words; the second doesn't know the joke but knows the standard dialogue, which goes as follows:

First person: Knock, knock!
Second person: Who's there?
First person: <Something>
Second person: <Something> who?
First person: <Punchline>.

For example:
Knock, knock!
Who's there?
Orange.
Orange who?
Orange you glad I knocked??

Here are some golden oldies, leaving out the first two sentences:
Police.
Police who?
Police let us in; it's cold out here!

Doris.
Doris who?
Doris locked, that's why I had to knock!

Tank!
Tank who?
You're welcome!

Boo.
Boo who?
Don't cry. It's just a knock-knock joke!

Woo.
Woo who?
Don't get so excited. It's just a joke.

Amos.
Amos who?
A mosquito bit me!

Andy.
Andy who?
Andy bit me again!

Dwayne.
Dwayne who?
Dwayne the bathtub! I'm dwowning!

Cargo
Cargo who?
Car go beep-beep!

Lettuce.
Lettuce who?
Lettuce in and you will find out!

Juicy.
Juicy who?
Juicy what I saw?

Ivan.
Ivan who?
Ivanna suck your blood!!

Little old lady.
Little old lady who?
Wow! I didn't know you could yodel.

Eurypides.
Eurypides who?
Eurypides pants,
you buy me some new ones!

Anita.
Anita who?
Anita go to the potty!

This one's for a quick trip down memory lane; today's kids won't get it!

Ice cream!
Ice cream who?
Ice cream of Jeannie!

You may even find yourself sharing this one with your adult friends.
Knock, knock!
Who's there?
Interrupting cow.
Interrupting cow who?
— but before they can finish asking, jump in with a loud *"MOO!"*

Farewell Rhymes

If you teach the kids these little rhymes, be prepared for long farewells — they'll want to run through the whole list.

See you later, alligator!
Toodaloo, kangaroo!
In a while, crocodile!
See you soon, baboon!
Take care, teddy bear!
Gotta fly, French fry!
Time to squirm, wiggle worm!
Let's scat, alley cat!
Better skadoodle, poodle!
Out the door, dinosaur!
Wave good-bye, butterfly!
So long, King Kong!
Goodbye, cow pie!

A few more short rhymes…
Give me a hug, ladybug.
Okeedokee, artichokee.
Good thinkin', Lincoln
Wrong-o, bongo!
Know what I mean, jelly bean?
Sure do, tennis shoe.

And, finally, this rhyme wraps up each long day of fun, when someone spots the first star of the night:

Star light, star bright,
First star I see tonight,
I wish I may, I wish I might,
Have the wish I wish tonight.

Index